LOOK INSIDE

# A VICTORIAN HOUSE

RICHARD WOOD
Illustrated by Adam Hook

WAYLAND

**Editor:** Jason Hook
**Series Design:** Ian Winton
**Book Design:** Jean Wheeler
**Cover Design:** Dennis Day

First published in 1998 by Wayland Publishers Ltd,
61 Western Road, Hove, East Sussex BN3 1JD, England
© Copyright 1998 Wayland Publishers Ltd.

Find Wayland on the Internet at http://www.wayland.co.uk

**British Library Cataloguing in Publication Data**
Wood, Richard, 1949-
    Look inside a Victorian House
    1.Dwellings - History - 19th century - Juvenile literature
    2.Architecture, Victorian - Juvenile literature
    3.Architecture, Domestic - Juvenile literature
    4.Interior decoration - Juvenile literature
    I. Title II. Victorian House
    392.3'6'009034

ISBN 0 7502 2283 2

Printed and bound in Italy by G. Canale & CSpA, Turin
Colour reproduction by Page Turn, Hove, England

**Cover pictures**: A Victorian family (centre); a smoking cap
(top); Mrs Beeton's cookery book (left); knife-cleaning
equipment (right).
**Picture acknowledgements**
The publishers would like to thank the following for permission
to reproduce their pictures (t=top; c=centre; b=bottom; l=left;
r=right): Beamish, North of England Open Air Museum *cover*
(c), 10b, 12l, 18c, 25t, 26c; Billie Love 8c, 10t, 19b, 24l;
Bridgeman Art Library, London/New York, /Science Museum,
London 8b, /Wimbledon Sewing Co., London 11b, /Christopher
Wood Gallery, London, UK 14l, /Fine Art Society, London 15t,
/Private Collection 24b; Christie's Images 23t; Getty Images 6t,
11tl, 15r, 28l; Mary Evans 7t; National Portrait Gallery 22c;
National Trust 4t, 6b, 21b, 26t, 29t; Norfolk Museums Service
*cover* (bl, br), 9b, 13t, 21r; Richard Wood 26b; Robert Opie 9r,
12b, 16, 20t; Science and Society 11tr, 12t, 17, 18b, 21t, 25b,
27r; Topham 4b, 13b, 14-15b, 20bl. All other photographs are
by Zul Makhida, Chapel Studios, reproduced courtesy of Royal
Pavilion, Libraries and Museums (Preston Manor), Brighton.

# CONTENTS

# HOUSE

## FIRST STIRRINGS

Take a look at a Victorian street. It is five o'clock in the morning. The lamplighter begins his round, putting out the flickering street lamps that have burned all night. Through the mist, you can make out the tall terraced houses. At some, the lamplighter taps on the windows with his pole to wake up the occupants. At others, a plume of smoke is already rising from the kitchen chimney.

▲ The London home of a famous Victorian writer called Thomas Carlyle.

You can still see terraced houses, like the one above, in towns and cities all over the country. In Victorian times, they were the homes of the better-off townspeople – 'respectable' families of shopkeepers, tradesmen, teachers and clerks. Richer people lived in larger, detached houses.

*'The Servants' Department shall be separated from the main house, so that what passes on either side of the boundary shall be both invisible and inaudible to the other.'* [1]

*(Sources for all quotes can be found on page 31.)*

◀ A middle-class family outside their house, in about 1890.

Many houses were three storeys high. Big city homes also had a basement, called the 'area', below ground level. Though space was limited, people tried to keep the working rooms of the house separate from the living quarters. A special door covered with green-baize cloth kept out the noise and smells of the kitchen.

Household Hints
If you do not rise early you can make progress in nothing. 2

▶ A cutaway showing the rooms of a Victorian house.

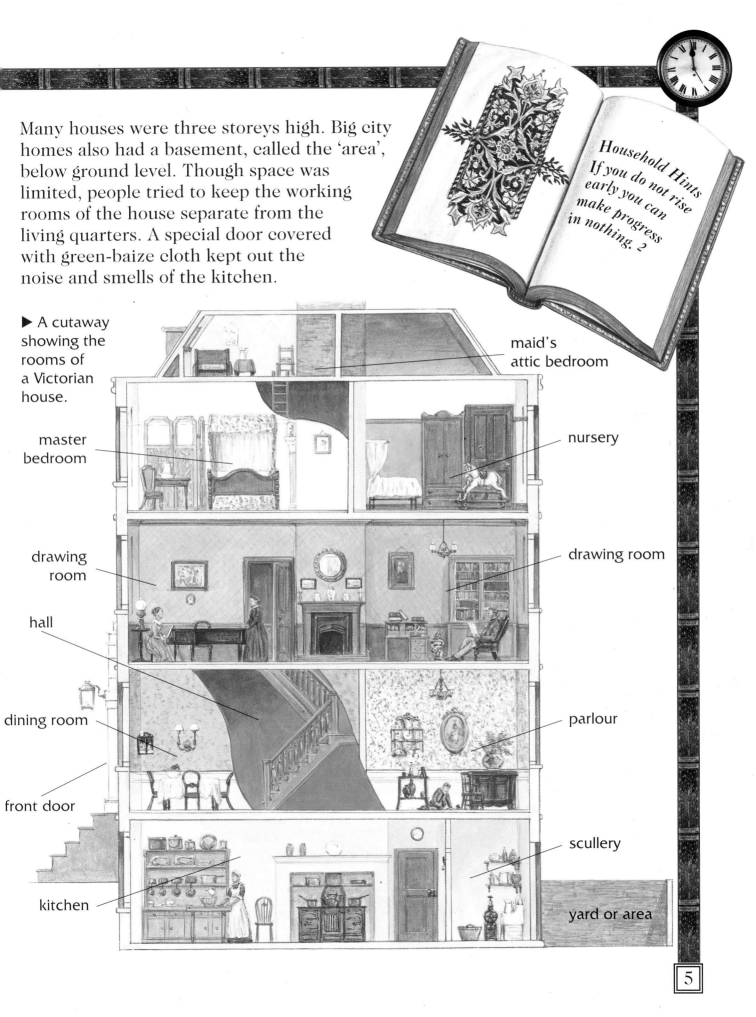

maid's attic bedroom

master bedroom

nursery

drawing room

drawing room

hall

dining room

parlour

front door

kitchen

scullery

yard or area

# SERVANTS' BELLS

## THE SUMMONS

There is a jangling of bells. 'Whatever now?' mutters Wilson the housemaid. She glances up at the bell board on the kitchen wall. The brass bell marked 'Drawing Room' is still swinging on its spring. Perhaps the mistress is preparing this room for her morning visitors. Maybe she wants more coal taken up. Whatever it is, the maid must hurry to see what her mistress wants.

▲ The mistress gives the maid her orders for the day.

The Victorian housewife was in charge of running the house. But the hard work of scrubbing, dusting, tidying, fire-lighting, washing, ironing and cooking was done by the servants.

For a middle-class family not to employ at least one servant girl was almost unthinkable. Wires hidden in the ceilings connected bell pulls in the main rooms to bells in the kitchen, so the servants could be summoned.

◀ The maid soon learned to recognize the different notes of the bells for each room.

Only rich families in grand, detached houses could afford to employ lots of servants. Most middle-class people made do with one 'maid of all work'. She was usually a teenage girl from a poorer family. The maid's day was long, lonely and exhausting. From lighting fires at 6 am to carrying hot water upstairs at bedtime, she had little rest.

▶ The first chore of the day was to polish the grates and light the fires.

*A woman's work is never done.* [3]

'Nothing annoys a mistress so much as to find, when she comes downstairs, articles of furniture looking as if they had never been dusted.' [4]

With no radiators or electric heaters, Victorian houses could be very cold. Open coal fires may look cosy, but they also create draughts and a lot of dust to clean up.

▲ A freshly polished copper coal scuttle and brass fire-tongs.

▲ The maid's box contained her cleaning materials, such as brushes and black-lead paste for polishing fireplaces.

# HASTENER

## KIDNEYS IN THE KITCHEN

'Curse you, old monster!' complains the maid. The iron cooking range is so hard to manage. Some days it blazes away almost out of control, others it just belches out clouds of smoke. Today, with the family sat at breakfast waiting for their kippers and kidneys, it is barely hot enough to melt the fat.

▶ The maid consults her *Mrs Beeton* while frying kippers.

▲ A Victorian family eating breakfast in the garden.

Most Victorian kitchens had coal-fired cooking ranges. From about 1850, a new sort of stove began to appear – the 'gas kitchener'. Early ones sometimes exploded, and people said they made the food taste strange. Not surprisingly, they were slow to catch on.

▶ An 1859 gas cooker. Many families rented a cooker rather than buying one.

The Victorians had some very curious kitchen contraptions. The 'hastener' was a rounded metal shield, placed in front of the open fire of a coal-burning range. Meat was hung inside, and rotated on a clockwork 'bottle jack'. The heat reflected by the shield 'hastened' or speeded-up the cooking.

◀ A hastener with a clockwork 'bottle jack'.

*Too many cooks spoil the broth.* 5

Middle-class Victorian families took food and cooking very seriously. They expected even plain family dinners to have several different dishes, all separately cooked and attractively served. New inventions appeared, including apple-peelers, ice-boxes, whisks and mixers, but cooking was still a time-consuming and sweaty task.

▲ A Victorian hand-powered food mixer.

'*Clear up as you go; muddle makes muddle.*' 6

In 1861, Mrs. Beeton's *Book of Household Management* was published. It contained recipes and advice on housework and the duties of servants. It became an instant best-seller, and was a vital part of many kitchens.

▲ Mrs Beeton's cookery book.

# SEWING MACHINE

## CRIMPERS AND CRINOLINES

It is 10 am, and the maid brings the morning mail in to the parlour. She waits by the door while her mistress opens and reads a grocer's bill, and an invitation to tea. 'Will that be all, Ma'am?' asks the maid. 'Yes, Wilson, but make sure you do not forget to iron the master's newspaper.'

*'The fair sex possess an unlimited stock of what we will term rubbish, such as ribbons, bows, sashes, gloves, mittens, etc. which are too good to throw away, and yet are much [too] faded, stained or soiled to be of use in their present condition.'* [7]

▶ A lady opening a letter in her parlour, in about 1880.

▲ Look at the draped mantelpiece in this parlour.

The rooms in the house, like most things in Victorian society, were divided between the sexes. The dining room was very masculine, painted in strong, dark colours. But the parlour was a ladies' room. It was decorated with flowery wallpaper and littered with little 'nick-nacks' and ornaments.

The parlour was the first room to be cleaned each day. Every morning, the maid was summoned there by her mistress. She was given her orders and had to help plan the menu for the day's meals.

Victorian ladies wore dresses with enormous 'crinoline' frames. These made it difficult to sit down or to manoeuvre past the carved furniture that filled the parlour. The crinoline sometimes caught alight if it brushed too close to the fire!

*The modern crinoline is absurd, dangerous, out of place and extravagant.* 9

◄ A dress is carefully lowered over a crinoline using special poles.

*'Shirt-making is quite easy, great care and neatness only being required.'* 8

▶ A crimping iron, for making ridged patterns on collars and cuffs.

In the parlour, a lady could read, entertain her children and sew. With a maid to do the chores, there was plenty of time for needlework. The parlour was adorned with examples of the mistress's handiwork. When sewing machines were invented, many women took up dress-making. They bought patterns and copied the latest fashions.

◄ A novelty sewing machine, made in 1893.

# MANGLE

## SCULLERY SCIVVIES

Today is washday. The scullery is so steamy that moisture trickles down the walls. A washerwoman helps Wilson with the weekly wash. She feeds sheets through the mangle, while Wilson presses 'smalls' with flat irons. The maid then grates soap into her washtub and complains: 'You know that old saying about the week's work being done by Thursday? Well, our work won't be!'

▲ An early washing machine with a mechanical dolly and mangle.

Traditionally, Monday was washday in a Victorian house. This allowed the rest of the week for drying, starching, ironing and airing the clothes. The washerwoman used a tub, a washboard (for rubbing out dirty marks) and a 'dolly'. This was a special pole which had three legs for turning the clothes around in a tub. Clothes were squeezed through a mangle to dry them.

◀ Two maids using a dolly and an iron.

▶ The flat iron (right) was heated on the range. The other iron was filled with hot charcoal.

'Keep your temper on washday. Washing must be done.' [10]

The scullery was at the back of the house between the kitchen and the yard. It was where the wet or dirty jobs were done. The scullery had a stone sink, a pump or tap, and a wooden washing-up bowl. There were no detergents. Grease had to be dissolved in strong soda, which left the poor maid's hands red raw.

*When Thursday's come, the week's work is done. 11*

Larger households employed a scullery maid just to do the dirty jobs. There were knives to polish, carpets to beat, ornaments to dust and doorsteps to whiten with a special brick. Most mistresses were very 'house proud'. They worried what their friends and neighbours would think if their homes were not spotless.

▲ Knife-cleaning equipment, for removing rust from iron blades.

▶ This vacuum cleaner from the early 1900s was one of the first electric models.

13

## THE CALLING CARD

**A**t 2 pm, the maid opens the front door to a tall lady wearing a shawl and bonnet. 'Is your mistress 'at home'?' the stranger enquires. Wilson hesitates, unsure whether her mistress is receiving guests. 'Oh, yes!' she remembers. 'Kindly step inside.' The lady hands Wilson two small, printed cards. The maid takes these upstairs while the visitor folds down her umbrella.

▼ A butler checks the calling cards.

▲ This umbrella stand was made from an old barrel.

Today, we might telephone before making a visit. Victorian visitors left calling cards instead. If the mistress was receiving visitors, she was said to be 'at home'. If she was not, the visitor left three cards. Two displayed her husband's name, and one showed her own name.

▲ Ladies kept calling cards in fancy cases.

▲ A girl hides from unfamiliar faces as her parents receive visitors.

The hall was the first part of the house seen by visitors. A mahogany table, carved chairs and an umbrella stand gave guests a good impression. From the hall, visitors were led to the parlour or drawing room. Only close friends stayed for more than fifteen minutes. Other callers did not remove their coats or bonnets.

▶ The maid wore her smartest dress on 'at home' days.

*Serious discussions are to be altogether avoided.* 12

'Visitors should refrain from bringing children. Besides often hearing much which they should not, they are apt to make awkward remarks.' 13

## THE THUNDER BOX

It is mid-afternoon. The cleaning is finished, fires are laid, and callers have left. Wilson puts on her special bedroom apron, and plumps up the feather beds. But whatever is this? Last night's slops and chamber pots have still not been emptied into the new water closet. She carries them carefully downstairs. Her mistress would not want spillages.

▼ Emptying chamber pots was not the favourite job of the day!

▲ Pretty, patterned potties were for grown-ups, plain ones for children and servants.

'How objectionable it is when a doorway in the vestibule fills the house with unwelcome odours.' 14

▶ A steriliser for disinfecting pots with strong chemicals.

Until the 1850s, people thought that disease was caught from breathing bad air. In poor areas, thousands died every year from illnesses such as typhoid fever, carried in polluted water. Better-off people used water purifiers and disinfectants.

By 1880, many large towns had piped water and sewers. At last it was possible to install a flushing toilet or 'water closet' in ordinary homes. Families did not want the toilet too close to their living quarters, so they installed it in a little room beside the scullery. Country people still made do with an outdoor 'thunder box'. This was a seat over a pit or bucket.

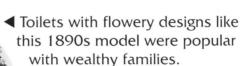

*Cleanliness is next to Godliness. 15*

◀ Toilets with flowery designs like this 1890s model were popular with wealthy families.

By the end of Queen Victoria's reign, the introduction of factory products made it easier to keep homes, and people, clean. Tins and bottles of special, ready-made polishes, powders, pastes and soaps brought a sparkle to everything from floor tiles to light fittings. You could even buy medicated toilet paper called 'curl papers'.

▶ Washing behind the ears, from a Pears Soap advert.

# TENNIS RACQUET

## GARDEN GAMES

'Papa, please let us go outside,' plead the children. 'Very well,' their father agrees, 'But if you are to play tennis, be sure to wear respectable, long dresses. And there's to be no skipping in the shrubbery or hoopla round the hotbeds.' Papa is proud of his garden and hopes his marrows will once again win first prize at the horticultural show.

◄ Victorian tennis racquets were less springy than modern ones.

▲ Croquet was a suitable game for small gardens.

The garden of a terraced house was usually narrow but long, with flower borders down each side. The lawn was cut short for games like croquet and tennis. At the bottom of the garden was a vegetable plot. This had manured 'hotbeds' and glass frames for growing tender plants like tomatoes, cucumbers and marrows.

▶ A hand-pushed lawn mower from about 1840.

◄ The gardener collects his employer's prize marrows.

*The possession of a quantity of plants does not make a garden. 16*

Gardening was a popular hobby for Victorian gentlemen. A part-time gardener was sometimes employed to tend to lawns and flower beds, and raise vegetables that might be prize-winners.

► Teatime in the garden complete with crockery and a fancy tablecloth.

Victorian families believed in plenty of fresh air and exercise to keep them healthy. In mild weather, they used the garden like an extra living room. They ate meals and entertained friends there. Some gardens also had a summer house or conservatory to provide extra warmth and shelter.

# BABY'S BOTTLE

## THE NURSERY

It is 5 pm. Martha Spratts, a nursemaid, is bathing the baby in the nursery. Martha is only fifteen, but she is used to looking after her own baby brothers and sisters. The nursery is on the top floor, so the baby's crying will not disturb the family. 'A place for everything, and everything in its place,' says a notice on the wall.

► An advert for Ridge's ready-made baby food.

▼ A leather or rubber teat fitted over the neck of this baby's bottle.

Natural breastfeeding of babies was frowned on by many Victorian mothers. They said that sort of behaviour was fit only for the farmyard! Milk and baby foods were fed to the baby instead, from glass bottles. Unfortunately, these were hard to clean, and many babies picked up infections from them and died as a result.

◄ This lucky baby has his bath in front of the parlour fire.

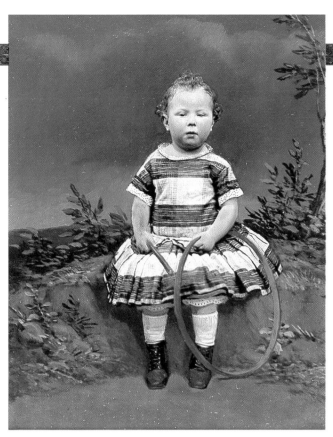

Children should be seen and not heard. 17

◀ A hand-tinted photo from about 1860.

Most toys in the nursery were home-made. Victorian parents believed in strict discipline and Christian worship, so toys had to be put away on Sundays. 'For bad boys,' one mother said, 'a yard of strap is worth a mile of talk.'

▲ A family of handmade wooden dolls.

'Prams are a public nuisance. They are wheeled against and between people's legs, and are a fruitful source of the breaking of shins, of the spraining of ankles, of the crushing of corns, and of the ruffling of tempers of all the foot passengers who come within their reach.' 18

◀ Prams allowed babies to share their parents' love of fresh air.

# GONG

## DINNER IS SERVED

At 8 pm, the maid bangs the dinner gong to summon family and guests to the dining room. In this household, dining is taken very seriously. With guests present, only the older children are allowed to attend. They are told never to speak unless spoken to.

▲ A large and noisy dinner gong.

▼ A grand dinner party in a rich household.

'How sad it is to sit and pine
The long half hour before we dine!
Upon our watches oft to look,
Then wonder at the clock and cook.' [19]

Several courses were served at a dinner party. Each had its own set of cutlery and was accompanied by a different wine. The master sat at the head of the table, and the mistress at the foot. The maid, in her best apron, waited on the guests.

In 'polite society', people followed strict rules when serving dinner. These rules changed in about 1860, when 'Russian service' became fashionable. Instead of all the dishes being placed together on the table, maids now offered them separately to every guest. Ladies and more senior gentlemen were served first, young men and children last.

'The vegetarian fad is mere twaddle, founded on an ignorance of nature.' 21

▲ A lively after-dinner entertainment for the gentlemen.

After dinner, the ladies withdrew to 'powder their noses' and take coffee in the drawing room. Before joining them, the gentlemen stayed in the dining room to smoke, discuss business or tell the sort of jokes ladies might not appreciate.

◀ A gentleman wore a smoking hat and jacket when smoking after dinner.

# PIANO MUSIC

## THE DRAWING ROOM

'Now, my dears,' says the mistress, 'Gather round the piano with your music.' The guests look at one another, no one wishing to be the first to perform. Secretly, though, everyone has practised a party piece for this moment.

▲ Songs for the piano.

The Victorians had no radio or television, so people made their own entertainment. After dinner, the family and their guests recited poetry, played music and enjoyed games like charades.

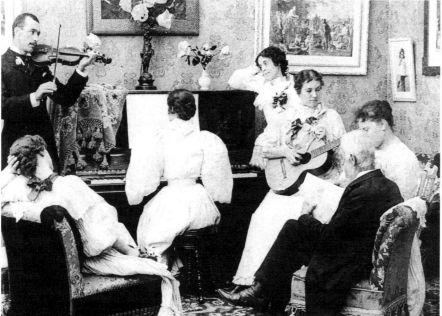

▲ Most people could sing or play an instrument.

The drawing room was so-called because it was for 'withdrawing' after dinner. It was more formally decorated than the parlour, with the best furniture and displays of tasteful ornaments. Some people covered up piano legs, because they thought bare legs were rude!

▶ Paperweights and domed figures were popular ornaments.

The drawing room should be planned to favour the forming of the company into separate groups. 22

▲ The family gather round the fireplace.

'There is nothing in the world more suggestive of home comfort than an English fire. The shabbiest furniture, the most homely surroundings gather new charms in the glow of a bright fire. A clean-swept hearth and dancing flames delight the heart of the tired home-comer.' 23

Victorian people loved pictures. They covered their walls with everything from large oil paintings in elaborate plaster frames to novelty items made from feathers and woodchips. Some people wallpapered only in the gaps between pictures. As photography became cheaper, family photos took pride of place.

▲ These photographs were taken in the 1840s.

## THE MASTER BEDROOM

It is 10 pm. A horse-drawn cab has already taken the dinner guests home and the fires are burning low. 'Time for sleep,' Papa calls to the children, as he winds up the grandfather clock on the landing. 'It's very late, so blow out the candles as soon as you've read your Bible.'

◄ Some first-floor landings had a grandfather clock like this one.

▼ Victorian beds had deep mattresses and many covers.

▲ There was always a danger that pottery hot-water bottles would leak.

DOULTON'S IMPROVED FOOT WARMER

LAMBETH POTTERY
LONDON

'In bedmaking, the fancy of the occupant should be consulted; some like beds sloping from the top towards the feet; others, perfectly flat; a good housemaid will accommodate each bed to the taste of the sleeper.' 24

◄ The master of the house winding the best clock.

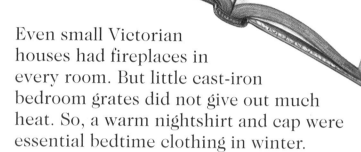

*Reading the Bible should have first place in all homes.* 25

Even small Victorian houses had fireplaces in every room. But little cast-iron bedroom grates did not give out much heat. So, a warm nightshirt and cap were essential bedtime clothing in winter.

*'The general servant deserves commiseration: her work is never done.'* 26

By 1890, electricity was available in some cities. But most people still relied on gas or oil for lighting. At night, the gas was turned off in case it leaked and caused an explosion. People burned 'night lights' – short candles in special holders – in case they needed a light in the middle of the night.

◄ Snuffers, for trimming candle wicks to stop them smoking.

▶ Oil lamps burned brighter than candles.

# TIN BATH

## THE MAID'S BEDROOM

It is 11 pm. Wilson has been on duty for nearly eighteen hours. 'Only one more job,' she sighs, staggering upstairs with a heavy china jug. There is no bathroom in the house. Water for the whole family is heated in kettles and carried upstairs, to fill bowls on the washstands in the family bedrooms.

▼ People bathed in their bedrooms in hip baths like this one.

*'Why should not servants have a neat and pretty room? It would be one means of civilizing them and improving their tastes. And surely they require baths even more than their mistresses do.'* 27

When they were not in use, tin baths were stored in the scullery or shed. A hip bath could be filled with only one jug of water. A full-sized tin bath required a number of jugfuls. Adults enjoyed hot baths in front of the kitchen range, but children usually had to bath in cold water.

◄ A weary housemaid. Her tight dress and stiff collar do not look comfortable.

▲ The back of Thomas Carlyle's house. You saw the front of his house on page 4.

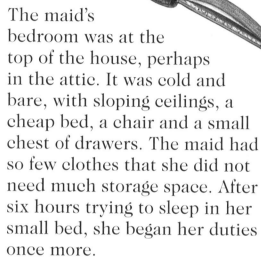

*Home is a sacred place, watched over by household gods. 28*

The maid's bedroom was at the top of the house, perhaps in the attic. It was cold and bare, with sloping ceilings, a cheap bed, a chair and a small chest of drawers. The maid had so few clothes that she did not need much storage space. After six hours trying to sleep in her small bed, she began her duties once more.

▼ The maid tries to enjoy her well-earned rest.

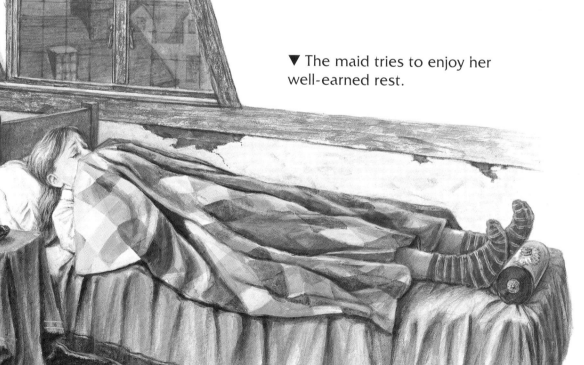

# GLOSSARY

**adorned** Decorated with ornaments to make more beautiful.

**airing** Warming washed laundry, to remove damp.

**apt** Likely.

**baize** Thick woollen cloth, similar to felt.

**best-seller** A book that sells a large number of copies.

**bottle jack** A bottle-shaped, clockwork machine for turning meat.

**charades** A game where people mime or act out a word or name.

**clerks** Office workers.

**commiseration** Feeling of sympathy or pity.

**crinoline** A bell-shaped frame worn under a dress.

**detached** Having no houses on either side.

**flat iron** An iron heated on a stove and used for pressing clothes.

**grate** Frame where fuel is placed for a fire.

**hoopla** A game where you throw rings over targets.

**horticultural** To do with gardening.

**hotbeds** Manured beds of earth for growing plants.

**inaudible** Unable to be heard.

**kippers** Smoked herrings.

**lamplighter** Someone paid to light and put out street lights.

**mangle** A machine with two rollers which squeeze clothes dry.

**mantelpiece** A wooden shelf above and round a fireplace.

**medicated** Containing substances that are good for health and hygiene.

**nick-nacks** Small, worthless ornaments.

**plumps up** Shakes and pats (a pillow) to loosen the feathers inside.

**range** An iron cooking stove heated by a coal fire.

**scuttle** A box or bucket for holding coal.

**slops** Dirty water from the kitchen and bedrooms.

**smalls** Underwear.

**soda** A strong chemical used for washing.

**starching** Applying starch, a substance which stiffens clothing.

**strap** A strip of leather used for beating naughty children.

**terraced** Having houses on either side.

**twaddle** Nonsense, useless writing.

**vestibule** A lobby next to the outside door.

**yard** A measure of length equal to just under one metre.

# FURTHER READING

## SOURCES OF HOUSEHOLD HINTS

1. *Hints on Household Taste* by Robert Kerr, 1868.
2. Lord Chatham.
3. Traditional.
4. *Book of Household Management*, by Mrs Isabella Beeton, 1861.
5. Traditional.
6. *Book of Household Management*.
7. An article in *The Lady*, 1889.
8. An article in *The Lady*, 1889.
9. *Book of Household Management*.
10. Traditional.
11. Traditional.
12. *Book of Household Management*.
13. *Etiquette of Good Society*, by Lady Colin Campbell, 1898.
14. *The Gentleman's House*, by Robert Kerr, 1864.
15. Traditional.
16. Gertrude Jeckyll.
17. Traditional.
18. *Counsel to Mothers*, by P.H. Chavasse, 1869.
19. Anonymous.
20. *Book of Household Management*.
21. *Self Help*, by Samuel Smiles, 1861.
22. John Stevenson.
23. An article in *The Lady*, 1885.
24. *Book of Household Management*.
25. *The Lady's Pictorial*.
26. *Book of Household Management*.
27. *Warne's Model Housekeeper*, 1879.
28. John Ruskin.

## BOOKS TO READ

*Changing Times, Housework* by Ruth Thomson (Watts, 1994)

*Daily Life in a Victorian House* by Laura Wilson (Hamlyn, 1993)

*Family Life in Victorian Britain* by Richard Wood (Wayland, 1994)

*Inside a Victorian House* by Dai Owen (National Trust, 1993)

*Investigating the Victorians* by Alison Honey (National Trust, 1993)

*The Victorian Household Album* by Elizabeth Drury and Philippa Lewis (Pargate Books, 1995)

*The Victorians at Play* by Rosemary Rees (Heinemann, 1995)

# INDEX